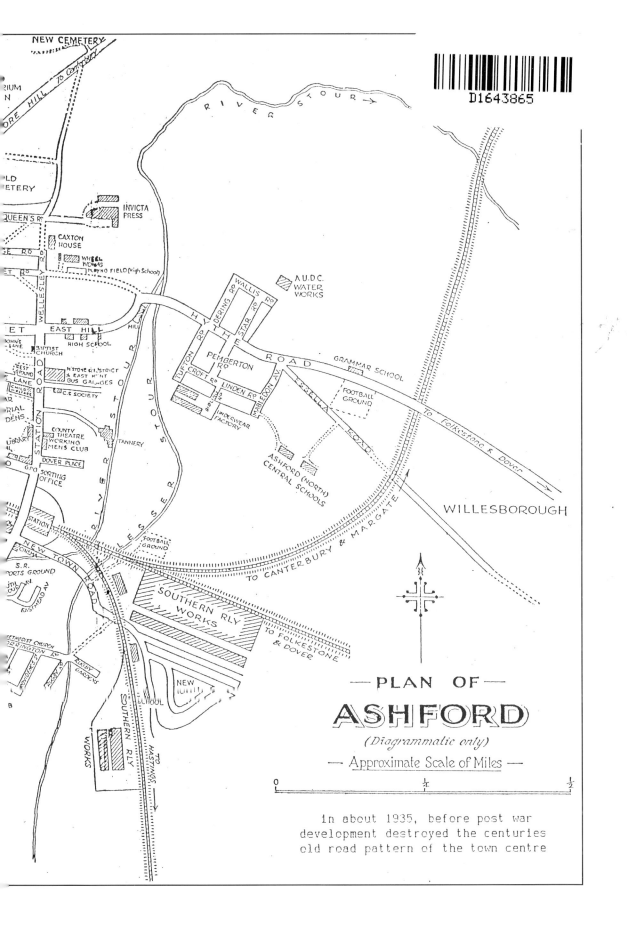

— PLAN OF —

ASHFORD

(Diagrammatic only)

— Approximate Scale of Miles —

0 ——— ¼ ——— ½

in about 1935, before post war
development destroyed the centuries
old road pattern of the town centre

ASHFORD
A Pictorial History

'The town of Ashford stands most pleasant and healthy on the knoll of a hill.' So wrote Edward Hasted, the Kentish historian, at the end of the 18th century. This print shows the town *c.*1840 with the uninterrupted view from the river before the building of the railway.

ASHFORD
A PICTORIAL HISTORY

Arthur Ruderman
&
Richard Filmer

Phillimore

1991

Published by
PHILLIMORE & CO. LTD.
Shopwyke Hall, Chichester, Sussex

ISBN 0 85033 802 6

Printed and bound in Great Britain by
BIDDLES LTD.
Guildford, Surrey

List of Illustrations

Frontispiece: Ashford *c*.1840

Acknowledgements

Most of the illustrations in this book come from the collection of Richard Filmer. They have been gathered over many years from many sources, and in some cases the original source and present ownership are unknown.

The authors wish to express their grateful thanks to those listed below, for their kindness and co-operation in making the photographs and other information available. The same thanks are expressed to anyone whose name does not appear, either because the source is unknown, or because of oversight.

Ashford Borough Council, Bill and Penny Broughall, Chartered Consolidated plc, Arthur Coleman, Adrian Coulling, Ronald Crosoer, Peter Fairman, Anna Flawn, Geerings of Ashford Ltd., Lewis Headley, Headley Bros. Ltd., Audrey Hughes, Kent Messenger Group, Norton Lee, James D. M. Mather, Vic Matthews, Nevill Norman, A. W. Palmer, Melanie Pentecost, Peggy Solomons, W. James Thomson, Bob and Jean Turner, John Watson.

Bibliography

Ashford: a Record of 500 years (1970)
Box, E. S., *Ashford Congregational Church* (1962)
Briscall, W., 'The Ashford Cage' in *Arch. Cant.*, Vol. 101 (1984)
Briscall, W., *Discovering Ashford's Old Buildings* (1987)
Filmer, R., *Old Ashford* (1983)
Filmer, R., *Ashford in Old Photographs* (1988)
Furley R., *Home Reflections* (1867)
Furley R., 'Early History of Ashford' in *Arch. Cant.*, Vol. 16 (1884)
Hasted, E., *History of Kent*, Vol. 7 (1798)
Hussey, A., *Ashford Wills, 1461-1558* (1938)
Igglesden, C., *Ashford Church* (1901)
Igglesden, C., *Saunter through Kent*, Vol. 34 (1946)
Ashford Local History Group, *Ashford's Past at Present* (reprinted 1982)
Ashford Local History Group, *Seventeenth Century Ashford* (1980)
Mills, M., *Doctor George Wilks* (1970)
Mortimore, E. T., *Sir John Fogge and Ashford Church* (1970)
Palmer, A. E. W., *History of Ashford Fire Brigade* (1987)
Pearman, A. J., *Ashford, its Church etc.* (1868, 1886 and 1904)
Rochard, J., *Ashford: Illustrated and Historical* (?1898)
St John's Ambulance, *Ashford Corps Centenary* (1979)
Thomas, R. W., *Sir Norton's School* (1980)
Toke, J., *Five Letters on the State of the Poor* (1808)
Turner, G., *Ashford: the Coming of the Railway* (1984)
Wallenberg, J. K., *Kentish Place-names* (1931)
Wallenberg, J. K., *Place-names of Kent* (1934)
Warren, W. M., *History of Ashford Church* (c.1712, printed 1895)
Watson, A. W., *History of Religious Dissent in Ashford* (1979)
Weeks, W. A., *Baptist Church of Ashford* (1931)
Wood, J. H., *The Martyrs of Kent* (1885)

Except for those published in the last few years, almost all of these books are out of print, but most can be seen in Ashford Library's Reference Room.

Introduction

Ashford was described by a journalist some years ago as a town without a history. For a place that is included in the Domesday Book of 1086 this is a surprising statement, and this is an attempt in a brief outline to correct that impression.

The name itself, given in old documents as *Esshetesford*, is of Anglo-Saxon origin and proves the existence of a settlement before the Norman Conquest. The meaning of the name is given by Wallenberg as 'the ford near a bend in the river, with ash trees'. Robert Furley, who was a solicitor and local historian living in Ashford in the last century, said that the ford in question was that at the bottom of East Hill on the road to Hythe, but this seems to be wrong. Lambarde, a 16th-century historian of Kent, says that the river was only called 'Stour' below Ashford, the name of the upper river being 'Eshet'. This is clearly the one which gave the town its name, but originally the two branches joined at the East Hill mill, and not by the station as they do now. That river which is now crossed on the approach to the Civic Centre was made in the medieval period to improve the flow of water to the mill, and until the last century was always described as 'the Lord's cut'. This means that the only ford on the Eshet was the one on the Beaver Road, just south of the station, and this must be the one that gave the town its name. The roads now known as Kingsnorth, Beaver and Station roads are the line of a road used by the Romans and also in medieval times, leading eventually to Canterbury. Anyone using that road would cross the river by a ford, and then find the river running parallel with the road – the bend mentioned in the name.

1. This view, taken at the beginning of this century, shows the extent to which the railway and the works created a barrier between the town and south Ashford, only to be crossed at a limited number of points.

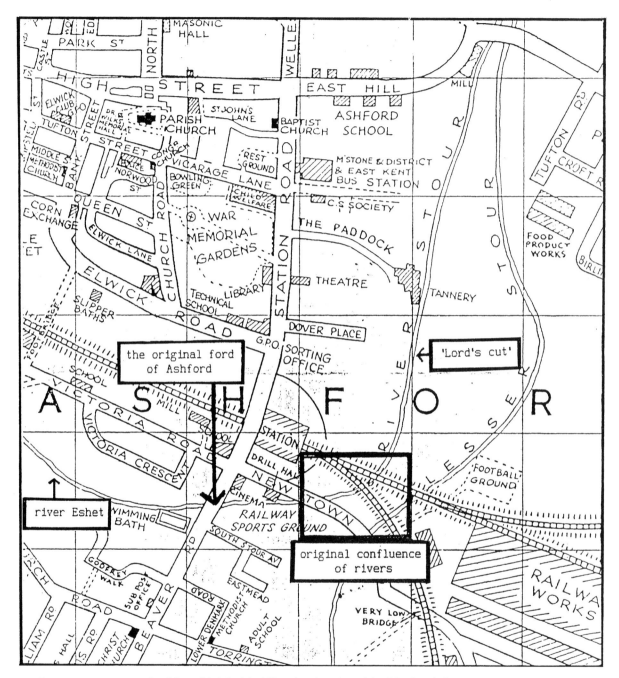

2. Map of Ashford in 1935, showing the original ford and river course.

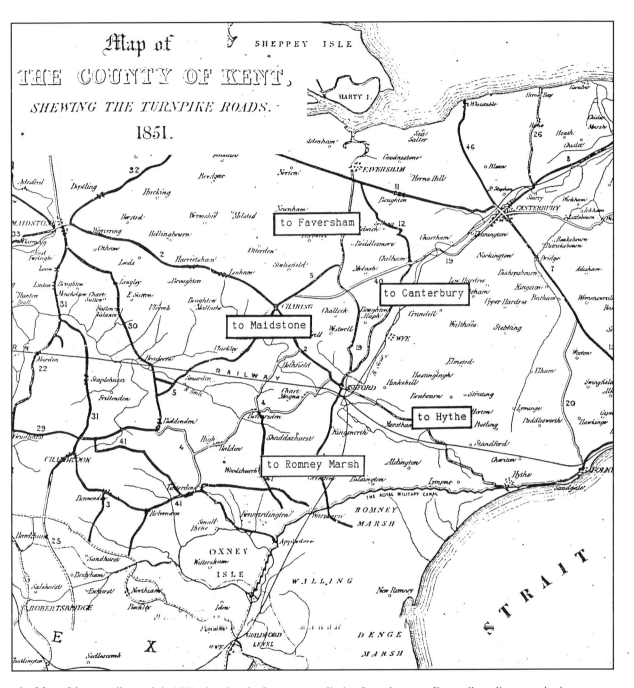

3. Map of the turnpike roads in 1851, showing the five routes radiating from the town. Four railway lines can also be seen; the fifth, to Maidstone, was not opened until 1882.

There must be good reasons for a town to prosper and expand. The two important factors in the case of Ashford are its position and the independent, if not rebellious, views of its inhabitants over the centuries.

Ashford is situated at a point where several routes cross. First is the route from the west leading from the south coast at Hastings and beyond to Canterbury, using the Stour valley – the only break in the hills in this part of Kent. Secondly there is the route running along the base of the Downs, leading to Maidstone in one direction and to Hythe in the other. The final route runs westward to the Weald via Tenterden. This was the last route to be developed, since until after the Conquest the forest of Anderida or the Weald stretched westward from Great Chart for well over 100 miles, and was for most purposes impenetrable.

The relative importance of the various routes in the 18th century is revealed by the dates when turnpike roads were authorised. Parliament allowed the levy of tolls on these important roads so that improvements could be carried out. The first (in 1762) was the route from Faversham to Ashford (via Challock). Despite the difficulties of Challock hill this was the route to London, either by road or water. It was also the road used for heavy goods such as coal, brought by sea and river to Faversham, and then by road. In 1762 the roads from Ashford to Canterbury and to Hythe were turnpiked, followed five years later by the road from Ashford to Tenterden. Not until 1793 were the roads from Ashford to Hamstreet and the Marsh, and the road to Maidstone turnpiked.

The town itself was in a good location on a hillside, with an adequate supply of water and of wood for fuel, and with good pasturage in the meadows on either side of the river. It is not surprising, therefore, that a market was established in Ashford at an early date. The first charter was granted to the lord of the manor in 1243. At that time the lord was Simon de Criol, who had obtained the manor through his wife Maud, daughter and heir of the last of a family known only as 'de Ashford'. That charter allowed for a weekly market on Saturdays, and an annual fair on the 'eve, day and morrow of the Decollation of St John the Baptist', that is 28, 29 and 30 August. Over the next centuries other lords obtained further charters to confirm or extend their rights. The manor extended over a large area, nearly 2,000 acres, including most of the town and South Ashford. In 1382 King Richard II granted the manor to the dean and canons of the Chapel of St Stephen in Westminster. They were probably responsible for major improvement works, including the building of a market house, and for the cutting of the channel to improve the flow of water to the mill at the bottom of East Hill.

A Custumal of 1514 sets out to clarify and define the rights of the lord in relation to the inhabitants. As a result, it was forbidden to fell large trees without the lord's permission and all houses had to be kept in good repair.

Following the upheavals of the Cromwellian period, the lord of the manor in 1675, Lord Strangford, thought it necessary to confirm his rights in a new charter. In 1784 the cattle market was established on a fortnightly basis, held (as no doubt the general market had been for centuries) in the lower High Street – the engraving by George Shepard of this scene in about 1830 is well known. The new site next to the railway was acquired in 1856, and the market transferred there. It has recently been decided that it should be moved again to an out-of-town site. When the market was first opened on the present site, that was described as 'out of town'!

Other areas specialised in particular types of trade. The butchers' stalls or shambles were in the narrow passages of Middle Row – on the side of the eaves gable of a shop facing North Street there can still be seen a carved badge with the initials 'JHS', those of John and Sarah Hills who lived there at the end of the 17th century. Another building in the middle of the High Street, opposite the Odeon, was once the butter market; this was demolished at the end of the 18th century. Corn was sold in the area to the east of the main block of buildings (now known as King's Parade) until the new Corn Exchange was built in 1856. Corn was also sold in a rival market established in the *Royal Oak*, in the lower High Street. The fish market was at the western end of the same block near the corner of Bank Street. As the town expanded, tradesmen such as carpenters, blacksmiths and saddlers, essential to a predominantly agricultural community, began to work in the town.

Inns opened to cater for the needs of both the residents and people coming to Ashford to trade. The brewing of ale and subsequently of beer, largely a domestic industry, goes back to very early times, but by the 16th century was both organised and controlled by the Justices. Most of the houses selling beer were quite small, and often only operated for a few years. There were also larger and more important establishments, providing not only meals and drink, but overnight accommodation. In Ashford the premier inn for many centuries was the *Saracen's Head*, in the High Street, near the corner with North Street. This was on land that belonged to the lord of the manor until the beginning of the last century, and may well have developed from accommodation provided originally for the steward of the manor when he came to collect rents and other dues. The half-timbered building that stood on the site for centuries was demolished *c.*1860, and this replacement building was in its turn pulled down in 1967 to make way for shops. For a very long time all important visitors stayed at the *Saracen's*, and it was also the venue for meetings such as the petty sessions.

The only important inn that still exists is the *George*. This dates from at least the 16th century and, like the *Saracen's*, was a coaching inn. Other important inns were the *Crown* in the lower High Street and the *Royal Oak* opposite, the *White Hart* (renamed the *Fountain* in the last century) in the upper High Street, and the *Red Lion* in North Street. All these have been demolished.

Ashford was designated a post town in 1677, enabling letters to be sent from and received in the town. At first the post came by horse via Maidstone, but by 1816 via Canterbury. At this time a letter for Charing had to go via Canterbury and Maidstone and, since the charge was calculated according to distance, this would be very expensive.

With the improvement of the roads, coach services developed and by 1830 Ashford was the centre of routes going to and from not only Hythe, Maidstone (and thus to London) and Canterbury but also villages over a wide area. The main routes were discontinued soon after the railway from London was completed in December 1842. Horse-drawn coaches and carts provided a network of services from villages to the nearest railway station.

Of other public services, gas for lighting was supplied from 1824, although there are many reports of complaints of bad service and the poor quality of the gas. After much argument the private company (which had become extremely profitable) was acquired compulsorily by the urban district council in 1899. Many attempts to provide an electricity service were made from 1882, but were opposed, and no public supply was available until 1926.

Water in the town centre was provided by a pump in the lower High Street, just above the Odeon cinema, and by many wells. In the middle of the 19th century a water company was formed to provide a piped supply. In 1868 it was agreed that a new pump was necessary in the High Street. A tender was accepted to provide this for £16 10s. 6d., but

10s. was to be saved by using the old handle! Water was pumped from the river at the bottom of East Hill; this was unsatisfactory since the town sewers discharged into the same river within a short distance. Unlike the gas company, the water company was anxious for the undertaking to be taken over by the council, but this was resisted for many years, and only in 1881 was the transfer made.

For centuries the effluent from the town had drained, without treatment, into the river. The sewer commissioners, responsible for the whole river Stour from Chart to the sea, were complaining of the nuisance as early as 1606, and by 1860, with the great expansion of population following the establishment of the railway works in 1847, the position had become intolerable. Sewers were provided from the 1860s, but these discharged raw sewage into the river near the mill. The question of providing some form of treatment works was considered by the local board of health from its foundation in 1863 for about twenty-five years. The townspeople rejected expert reports which said that the high incidence of disease was due to the lack of sewage works, and the arguments went on. It is clear from the newspaper reports that several members of the board considered they knew more than the engineers who were engaged to advise. Finally a contract was accepted in September 1887 to erect the works at Bybrook for the sum of £6,180. The editorial in the *Kentish Express* stated in the debate of 4 January 1865 that 'Ashford should wait, to profit by the experience of other towns before adopting any plan for preventing the pollution of the river. It cannot be said that the advice has not been followed'. The paper estimated that the cost of abandoned plans and legal expenses was at least £2,500!

Another development important to the commercial life of the town was banking. The first bank was opened in 1791 by George and William Jemmett (two members of the family which shortly afterwards took over the lordship of the manor), in partnership with Lewis Whitfeld. Opened at 24 North Street, the bank soon moved to 83 High Street, and by about 1850 was established at 81 High Street. It was absorbed by Lloyds Bank in 1901; their branch still operates from the same site. Another private bank was started in 1810, called Ashford Commercial Bank, but only survived for a few years. A trustee savings bank (one of the earliest in the country) was started in 1816.

The coming of the railway consolidated Ashford's position as a centre of communication in east Kent. The South Eastern Company built the first line to London, originally running via Tonbridge and Redhill, from where the tracks of the Brighton line were used. The station was opened on 1 December 1842, and within the next 10 years not only the main line to Folkestone and Dover was completed, but also the branch lines to Canterbury and Margate and across Romney Marsh to Hastings. Not until 1882 did the London and Chatham Company complete the line from Maidstone to Ashford. At that time this did not connect with the main line, and a separate station (Ashford West) was provided. Some of the buildings still exist as part of the goods depot.

Even more important was the decision by the South Eastern Company to establish their main workshops in Ashford, which completely altered the character of the town. There was an enormous increase in population, from under 3,000 in 1841 to nearly 13,000 in 1901. Ashford was transformed from a town dependent largely on its agricultural market into an industrial town, with a large proportion of the population dependent, directly or indirectly, on the railway for its livelihood. This remained the position until the middle of the present century, when the imminent decline of the railway led the district council to encourage the promotion of new opportunities for employment. The railway company did not simply build the works; they were responsible for the area at first named 'Alfred', but soon known to everyone as Newtown. They erected houses, a school, shops and a public house, and contributed to the cost of Christchurch, South Ashford.

The building of the M25 motorway, the channel tunnel and the associated railway seems likely to ensure the continued importance of Ashford into the 21st century and beyond.

4. The bridge on the Beaver Road, photographed *c*.1972. Variously known as Beaver bridge, the Stone bridge, or Trumpet bridge, it crosses the river at the same point as the original ford that gave the town its name. In the 18th century there was an inn nearby called the *Trumpet*. This probably explains the alternative name for the bridge, although it is not known whether the inn was named after the bridge or the other way round.

The good communications of Ashford with the surrounding area have led to a military presence at most times.

In the Elizabethan period we read of a meeting of the Queen's advisors at Ashford concerning the establishment in various places of facilities for the training of harque-busiers (an early form of portable gun). At this period all men were liable for service in an emergency, and were required to be proficient with the bow. The land immediately south of Tufton Street, including that now occupied by the police station and magistrates' court, was used as butts, where shooting was practised.

From time to time musters were called, at which all men had to report for training and is in keeping with the general attitude of men of Ashford that some did not comply – in 1635 the Justices were reporting the names of those who had failed to appear when called.

During the Civil War and for the rest of the century there are many reports of troops of men being stationed at Ashford. These were increasingly used not for defence against a possible foreign invasion, but to combat the activities of smugglers. This was specifically mentioned in a report of 1698, when they were ordered to assist the civil officers and magistrates in preventing the transportation of wool. This need was to continue for the whole of the 18th century, but without a great deal of success. These troops faced much difficulty in enforcing the law against the export of wool without licence, not least from the involvement of prominent men in the trade. Recent research has shown that Isaac Rutton, a doctor of medicine who lived in Ashford (in a house on the site now occupied by Lloyds Bank) was the leader of a gang of smugglers called the *Seasalter* gang. At the same time he was a respected local physician, a justice of the peace and a substantial landowner, his wife being a daughter of Toke of Godinton. One of his sons was rector of Badlesmere and another went to live at Ospringe. It is thought that they were involved too, and that their residences were strategically placed to serve as staging points from the north Kent coast to Maidstone and London.

For nearly 50 years the forces at home were at a very low level, but in 1859 it was decided that corps of volunteers should be established in the larger towns. A company was formed in Ashford in 1860, under the command of William Pomfret Burra (of the Ashford Bank), who was a marksman of national repute. In 1888 this company was able to lease a new drill hall erected in Norwood Street.

During the First World War many troops were stationed in the town before being moved to France, or after their return. There were at least two air raids, but little damage was caused.

Ashford again became a key point during the last war, and if an invasion had been made would have been a strongly-defended garrison. Defences were installed, particularly along the river banks that, it was hoped, would have enabled the town to resist tank attacks. Many of the civilian population were evacuated, and as many as possible of those remaining would have left had an invasion actually been launched. Fortunately this did not happen, and in due course the defensive works were dismantled. The town was, however, attacked on many occasions from the air, many houses being destroyed or damaged. In total air raid warnings were given on 2,869 occasions.

Another factor which has influenced the development of the town is the independent nature of its inhabitants. In the 13th and 14th centuries the 'King's peace' was not acceptable to many of the barons and great landowners who were quite prepared to take the law into their own hands if they thought it to their advantage. They headed bands of armed men who were ordered to carry out raids on neighbours. Armed conflict and mock-battles, such as tournament and jousting, were a way of life. Sir Roger of Leybourne (who acquired the manor of Ashford in 1271) was well known for his active hostility, and before King Henry III went abroad in 1262 he issued mandates forbidding him to attend tournaments. Nevertheless, the following year Sir Roger went to the aid of Sir William of Detling, who had been accused of homicide. Together they forcibly ejected the officers of the Archbishop of Canterbury who had been sent to take possession of the manor of Detling. Although the names of individuals are not recorded, the supporters of Roger would have come from his manors and may well have included men from Ashford. Roger de Leybourne almost certainly died in the Middle East whilst on the first crusade.

In the following century the first uprising by the general populace took place. In the Peasants' Revolt of 1381, provoked by the imposition of a poll tax, no Ashford names are recorded, although violent assaults on men and property occurred as near as Boughton Aluph and Wye. Amongst those charged were John Henwoode and Stephen Repton, both from families connected with Ashford.

The town's involvement with the rising of Jack Cade in 1450 is well documented, including the references in Shakespeare's *Henry VI*. Amongst the rebels he names Dick, a butcher of Ashford. He was obviously not at all friendly towards the legal profession, suggesting that (after the revolt had been successful) their policy should be 'let's kill all the lawyers'. The list of those pardoned after the successful revolt includes seven men described as being 'of Ashford'.

During the following years local men took part in the Wars of the Roses. John Fogge of Repton was at all the important battles, those of Northampton, St Albans and Towton. Although earlier a supporter of Henry VI (and appointed to lead the official opposition to Cade), he later supported Edward IV, being married to the cousin of Elizabeth Woodville, Edward's wife. The men of Ashford, led by Fogge, were almost certainly involved in these conflicts.

Individual opposition to authority begins with the religious controversies that led first to the Reformation and later to the Civil War.

Although religious views at variance with those of the established Catholic Church originated in the late 14th and the 15th centuries with the activities of John Wycliffe and later the Lollards, the first recorded instance in Ashford involves John Brown. He was brought before the Church courts in 1511 and, not being willing to recant his religious views, was burnt at Ashford on Whit Saturday 1517. From that time on Ashford became known as a centre for Protestant and puritan belief. John Ponet was appointed vicar in 1547; he was a known Protestant who fled to Strasbourg during the reign of Queen Mary. During her Catholic reign five Ashford men were burnt at Canterbury as Protestants.

In 1581 Joseph Minge was appointed as vicar. He was another confirmed Protestant, one writer claiming, 'hath not Minge brought Ashford from being the quietest town in Kent to be at deadly hatred and bitter division?'. Minge refused to subscribe to the Articles of Archbishop Whitgift, and would certainly have been punished by the Church courts if he had not died before procedures could be put in motion.

From then on there are many references to the involvement of Ashford people in the growing religious controversies. There are reports of early Baptists and Independent congregations in the town and in 1635 Archbishop Laud ordered Sir Edward Dering (as a Justice of the Peace) to take action against John Fenner of Egerton 'carpenter and pailmaker ... for being himself a schismaticall recusant and a Separatist'. Fenner was charged with others for heretical activity in the Ashford area.

In 1643 the vicar John Maccuby was ejected, and replaced by a puritan, John Boden. He was succeeded in 1647 by Nicholas Prigg. During this time the altar and altarpiece were removed and the church generally made plainer to conform to puritan beliefs. This was carried out by the churchwardens Joy Starr and William Worsley, but must have been supported by a majority of the population. The altar was not restored until 1697.

After the Restoration of Charles II in 1660, the dissenting congregations had to worship secretly, but Nicholas Prigg, ejected from the parish church, became the first minister of the Independent chapel, and there were Baptist and Quaker congregations at this time. They were not allowed full freedom of worship until William of Orange became William III in 1689. In December 1688 Sir John Knatchbull recorded in his diary that he 'went to Ashford and sent for the Chief of the Town and told him ... that it was very hazardous to us and to the Prince's cause to declare for him out of season'.

With the coming of the 18th century, religious controversy declined and the thoughts of the townspeople turned to more practical affairs. Nevertheless, many nonconformists continued to reside in the town as shown by the statements of the churchwardens in 1716 when applying for permission to increase the seating available in the church. This was said to be necessary to provide accommodation for those 'frequenting Presbyterian,

5. This photograph, also taken at the beginning of this century, shows North Street and the view to the Downs. There was little development beyond Queen's Road, and the town was separated from Kennington by a mile or two of open countryside. The building in the foreground, with poles and insulators on the roof, is 2 Middle Row, used from 1897 as the telephone exchange of the National Telephone Company. Their directory for 1897 listed nine subscribers in Ashford.

Independent and other Meetings' because of lack of space in the parish church.

Over the next two centuries there were many changes in public administration and in these Ashford was to be well in advance of many other areas. Poor relief had been a matter of great concern since the reign of Henry VIII, and various solutions had been tried over the years. In 1705 the parish sought permission of the Justices for the appointment of a workhouse keeper, having provided a workhouse. Although this had been done in other parts of the country, there was no general legislation to authorise it. Only in 1724 did Sir Edward Knatchbull, then one of the Members of Parliament for Kent, successfully promote such a bill, presumably aware of the success of the Ashford institution.

There was growing concern nationally in the second half of the 18th century over the problem of poor relief. John Toke of Godinton, Sheriff of Kent in 1770, circulated a number of open letters setting out his views on the necessary reform. New and strict workhouse rules, based on Toke's ideas were adopted in Ashford in 1770, the prime mover being Henry Creed, a draper. His views were not accepted by all; Thomas Waterman noted in his vestry book, 'seen and disapproved of every particular part of this Plan, and think Mr. Creed an unfit person to have anything to do with the Parish of Ashford'. The

6. Godinton House, the home of the Toke family from the 15th to the 19th century.

rules adopted were very harsh, and were reinforced when Ashford replaced the 'open' vestry that had managed the poor laws by a 'closed' vestry. Under this system, voting by ratepayers was proportional to the rateable value of the property they occupied. This, of course, gave greater power to the wealthier ratepayers who insisted on more control and restriction of expenditure. In a report written in 1834, the vestry was congratulated on having reduced expenditure on poor relief from £1,192 in 1822 to only £437 in 1832. It is unlikely that those who had been in receipt of relief shared this enthusiasm! The methods of the Ashford authorities were similar to those proposed by the Poor Law reforms of 1834. Because of this Ashford parish was at first excluded from the provisions of the Act, which established the Union workhouse at Hothfield. Ashford petitioned to be included in the scheme from 1836.

7. The badge and chain of the office of Mayor of the Borough of Ashford, formed after the local government re-organisation of 1974, by which the borough of Tenterden, the urban district of Ashford and the rural districts of East and West Ashford and Tenterden were merged.

Henry Creed was also active in promoting the scheme to pave the streets in Ashford. In many towns of Kent (and elsewhere) it had been found necessary to introduce a local Act of Parliament to appoint Commissioners to carry out this work. In Ashford the cost was met by public subscription.

A volunteer fire brigade existed from at least 1810, since it was reported to the Poor Law Commissioners in 1839 that 'the fire engine had been kept in the workhouse for upwards of thirty years'. The brigade was reorganised and new rules adopted in 1826. This was for many years thought to be the first in the country, but recent research has shown that the brigade at Hythe was founded in 1802.

During the late Victorian period it was proposed on several occasions that the town should apply for the status and powers of a municipal borough, with the right to appoint a mayor. This was opposed on the grounds of the cost involved. Not until after the reorganisation of local government in 1974, when the new district covering a much wider area was formed, did Ashford become a Borough with its own mayor.

ROADS

8.   Despite the number of turnpike roads, there were only three tollhouses within the parish; of these, no picture has been found of the one on the Tenterden Road near Chart Leacon. Shown in this photograph is the tollhouse on the Maidstone Road at Potters' Corner, at the beginning of the century. This is the only tollhouse still existing, now used as a private house.

9.   The original tollhouse on the road to Romney Marsh was at the bottom of Station Road (then called Marsh Lane). Just north of the station, it had to be moved near to the junction with Bond Road when the railway was built. This photograph of the tollhouse and the keeper was taken *c*.1870.

10.   After the turnpikes there was very little new road construction until the arrival of motorways. The building of a bypass for Ashford was planned well before the last war but not finished until 1957. The photograph shows the stretch near the Willesborough mill, now part of the M20, under construction.

11. Demolition and change is nothing new. This picture, dating from the end of the last century, shows substantial alterations in progress to nos. 74 to 78 High Street.

12. This view is of the *Duke of Marlborough*, on the corner of East Hill and Wellesley Road but demolished for the ring road, under repair at the beginning of this century.

13. Most of the houses in this photograph still stand, but the point from where it has been taken, *c*.1900, is now in the middle of the ring road at the junction with Canterbury Road. The unsurfaced road can be seen clearly – dusty in summer and a quagmire in winter.

14. At important points a stone causeway was provided to allow pedestrians to cross without walking in the mud. This view shows such a pathway, in Middle Row at the end of the last century.

15. Pavements for pedestrians were provided in the town centre at the end of the 18th century, but the roadway remained unsurfaced until the beginning of the present century. This photograph of North Street, taken *c*.1870, shows the poor conditions. Street lighting was introduced *c*.1825, at first with oil lamps but later by gas lighting when the first gasworks opened in Station Road in 1835.

16 & 17. These two photographs show North Street at the turn of the century and some forty years later. Little change is apparent, apart from the vehicles. In the last 20 years the *Lord Roberts* Inn (in earlier centuries the *Red Lion*) and several other buildings have been demolished.

18.   A view of the upper High Street at the turn of the century, showing the road surface.

19 & 20. This photograph and the next were taken with a panoramic camera, which enabled a much wider view to be taken, although with some distortion at the extreme edges. They show the upper High Street and Middle Row, at the beginning of this century.

21.   Another view of the upper High Street, taken *c*.1930. Clearly, although cars are becoming more usual, cycles are still being used by a large number of townspeople.

10. – High Street, Ashford.

22 & 23.   The houses in the above view taken looking up Castle Street, *c*.1905, were demolished at the beginning of this century in order to improve the road junction; the lower photograph shows the result, *c*.1920. It was this work which created the Square, where the tank was stationed in 1919.

24 & 25.   These two views are of Bank Street at the turn of the century. The construction of the railway works in 1847 and the consequent increase in population led to the demand for improved services in the town. At about the same time the more prosperous tradesmen were not content to live over the shop, as their forefathers had done, but demanded new residential areas. Church Road and Queen Street were built from about 1850, and then, from 1855, Bank Street. The Jemmett family owned a great deal of the land between the town and the railway, and this was developed by the construction of Bank Street, the lower part of which was originally called George Street.

26. The eight imposing villas in Elwick Road, seen here *c*.1870, were erected in 1865 by George Elliott, who lived in one of them himself. The house on the corner of Church Road called 'the Cedars' was used by departments of the Urban District Council from 1940 until the Civic Centre was built.

27 & 28. These two views are of Elwick Road at the turn of the century.

BRIDGE STREET

29 & 30.   Much of the land in south Ashford was liable to flooding from one or other of the branches of the river Stour, as can be seen in these photographs taken at the beginning of this century. This was only one of many floods. In November 1865 the *Kentish Express* reported that 'the dwellers in Goldmead Street (later Bridge Street) had to beat a retreat to the upper storey, and the occupant of one house found it necessary to remove his pigs from the garden and take them with him into the bedroom to save them from being drowned'.

THE MARKET

31. The market was undoubtedly held in the lower High Street from a very early date. In the 14th century the then lords of the manor, the dean and canons of the King's Chapel of Stephen in Westminster, were probably responsible for building a market house in the middle of the High Street – now 1 Middle Row, and seen in the centre of this photograph.

32. There were temporary trading places in the High Street until the early 16th century, when a new market hall with a court house on the first floor was built, as shown in this old print.

33. Ashford had one of the earliest organised volunteer fire brigades. This interesting illustration of 1897 was probably taken immediately after the purchase of the new steamer in celebration of Queen Victoria's Diamond Jubilee. The photograph is a little unusual insomuch as it was taken from the southern side of what we now know as Kings Parade, a narrow street which makes photography difficult. Several of the firemen can be identified, including (in front in the peaked cap) Captain F. S. Hart.

31. The old courthouse and the adjoining shops, taken *c*.1972, were acquired by the Urban Council in 1924 and the western end converted into offices, with a council chamber on the first floor.

35 & 36. This narrow passage was the Shambles, housing butchers' shops. The shield shown with the letters 'JHS' can still be seen on the side of 2 Middle Row. The initials are those of John and Sarah Hills. John was a butcher in the 17th century.

37.   The drawing for this engraving was made by George Shepherd. It shows well the confusion of Ashford market, being held in the lower High Street, *c*.1830, and the disturbance caused by the large number of people and animals.

38. The lower High Street about a hundred years later. Many of the buildings can still be recognised, though modern shopfronts have been added.

39. A modern view of the houses in the narrow part of the High Street backing onto the churchyard. The shop on the right of the photograph with the gable end is one of the oldest in the town, and belonged to Dame Alice Fogge, wife of Sir John who rebuilt the church tower, at the beginning of the 16th century.

40 & 41. In the middle of the last century it was felt that the market should be moved, both to reduce the nuisance and to provide more space. This move was not without opposition, but eventually a company was formed (one of the earliest limited companies allowed by the Companies Act of 1855) and the market moved to the new 'out of town' site next to the railway. The land was owned by George Elwick Jemmett, then lord of the manor, and the agreement included the transfer of manorial market rights under the ancient charters. The first market was held at the new site on 29 July 1856. These two views show the market at the beginning of this century.

42. Ashford market is particularly known for its sheep sales, with sheep coming from a wide area, but especially from Romney Marsh. This photograph shows a sale in progress.

43. Other livestock and a wide range of general goods are sold at the market.

44 & 45. After the market had been moved from the High Street there was a proposal to move the corn market to a nearby site. This also caused much controversy, but eventually this new Corn Exchange was erected at the bottom of Bank Street, opposite the market. It was opened in 1861 and was also the venue for all sorts of public gatherings – seating could be provided for between 800 and 1,000 people. These two pictures show the front and back of the Corn Exchange. The imposing columns were demolished when the building was altered and extended in 1904. It was demolished in 1965.

46. During the first half of the 19th century there were rival corn markets in Ashford. One was held in the public rooms in Middle Row, the other in the *Royal Oak* in the lower High Street. The photograph shows this inn, probably *c.*1880.

47. Corn dealing in progress in the early 1950s.

48. One of the trade exhibitions held at the
Corn Exchange at the beginning of this century.

49. There can be no doubt that the mill at the
bottom of East Hill is the successor to the one in
Domesday Book, although there must have been
many rebuildings over the centuries. This
painting shows the mill c.1916.

50. In about 1850 water for the town supply was pumped from the river at the same point and, as the photograph above left shows, new mills were erected in 1901.

51. Lawrence Pledge, above right, a member of the family which owned this and other mills at the beginning of this century.

52. The view on the left shows an early 19th-century windmill which was erected at the top of the town in Regent's Place. It was demolished c.1870.

SHOPS AND SHOPKEEPERS

53. There is always a need for food shops, and many grocers worked from the same premises for many years. This photograph shows Henry Headley who came to Ashford *c*.1847, and took over the grocer's shop at 38 High Street which had been run by William Jeffery for at least the previous 25 years. In 1860 Headley took over the old-established grocery business of Scott at 46 High Street and the business operated from there until it closed in 1976.

54. Headley's shop front at the beginning of this century.

W. F. HARVEY & SON,

Family Grocers & Provision Merchants,

GROCERY STORES,
2, HIGH STREET, ASHFORD.

Branches: 28, Beaver Place and 54 & 56, Torrington Road,
SOUTH ASHFORD.

TRY OUR OWN BLENDED TEA, 1/6 & 1/8.

55 & 56. 2 High Street was also a grocer's for a very long time. Early in the last century the occupier was William Sims, followed (*c.*1875) by William Fowler Harvey and his son. Just after the First World War the business was acquired by Pearks Dairies Ltd.

57. Grocers in the 19th century sold a wide range of goods. William Morley was a tallow chandler and maker of candles in addition to selling groceries. His shop was at 62 High Street (with bow windows on the upper storeys at the right of this photograph) until 1858, when he moved to new premises at 5 Bank Street. The High Street shop continued as a grocer's, until acquired by Boots the Chemists c.1914.

58. A year or two later the business in Bank Street was taken over by John Broad, who remained there until 1874. Broad then had a factory in Park Street, where the smell from melting fat provoked many complaints from nearby residents. The drawing of the shop shows that the scope of the business was being widened still further. Petrol became available (for lighting) c.1860.

Sole Agent
for
PETROL.

Agent for
Strange's
A 1 Oil.

59.   An early 20th-century photograph of Broad's shop.

60-62.   Another trade that flourished from an early date was that of draper. The shop on the corner of High Street and North Street was occupied by Thomas Apsley, a draper, from early in the 18th century, and has been used for related trades ever since. For much of the last century the draper was Benjamin Thorpe, followed by his son Benjamin Kelly Thorpe. Thomas Coulthard was in partnership with Arthur Parroch from about 1870, until 1885. He then continued on his own until 1903, when he became bankrupt. The photograph of the premises when he was there (right) can be compared with more recent views (below).

63. George Alexander Lewis was also a draper. He was a native of Tunbridge Wells who came to Ashford *c.*1838 to take over a long established draper's shop, previously run by John Rogers, at the top of New Rents. This picture was woven in pure silk and was a souvenir of the Trades' and Inventions' Exhibition held at Ashford in 1894.

64. Lewis's shop at the top of New Rents, on the corner with Forge Lane, photographed in 1972.

65. Lewis was a man of great ambition and later had premises extending down most of New Rents, as can be seen in this turn-of-the-century photograph.

66. Lewis extended gradually as property became available. This was revealed during demolition in the 1970s; the sign on the side of these buildings must have been painted before the erection of the tall building seen above. Later Lewis went into partnership with Frederick Hyland and had shops not only in Ashford but in other towns in Kent and East Sussex.

67 & 68.   Lewis also had a men's tailors at 93 High Street, which can be seen in these views, the one above at the beginning of this century, and the one below in 1972, with placards in the windows announcing the closure of the shop. Subsequently it was demolished to make way for the Tufton Centre.

69-71. Blacksmiths provided an essential service. There were several forges in Ashford including one at the top of St John's lane, which was owned by the Flint family from the middle of the 17th century; they were also braziers and ironmongers, with premises at 35-7 High Street (where the Odeon now stands) and seen on the left of the photograph above. The business passed to Edward Chittenden and then in the 1830s to John Dungey. He made railings to the churchyard, which bore his name, but these were recently replaced. By 1855 James Udal Bugler had bought the business. Towards the end of the last century the ironmongery business and foundry were split, the latter being taken over by George Mather (below right). Since 1922 the foundry has operated from a new site at Cobbs Wood. The ironmongery business was taken over by Alfred Olby Ltd., who moved to 5 High Street (the old *Royal Oak*).

No. 13, New Street, and Gilbert Road, Ashford.

Mr F Headley

Bought of William Ball,

WHOLESALE AND RETAIL

BASKET & SIEVE MANUFACTURER.

WOODWARE, COOPERAGE, & BRUSH WAREHOUSE.

CORN MEASURES, BUTTER CHURNS, BRINE TUBS, WOOD BOWLS, STRINGS, TWINES AND CLOTHES LINES, WASH LEATHER, SPONGE, &C.

Baskets Neatly Repaired.   Wicker, Rush, and Cane-seated Chairs Bottomed.

1873

May 24   3 Cane Chairs Bottming 1/4   4

72. Until the introduction of cheap wooden boxes, baskets were widely used for the storage of a wide range of dry goods. Prominent among basket manufacturers in Ashford were John Clover (at the beginning of the last century), then John Harper and, from *c.*1856, William Ball. Ball's invoice shows a wide range of products as well as baskets.

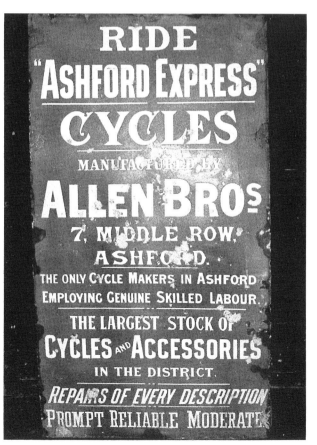

RIDE
"ASHFORD EXPRESS"
CYCLES
MANUFACTURED BY
ALLEN BROS
7, MIDDLE ROW,
ASHFORD.
THE ONLY CYCLE MAKERS IN ASHFORD
EMPLOYING GENUINE SKILLED LABOUR.

THE LARGEST STOCK OF
CYCLES AND ACCESSORIES
IN THE DISTRICT.
REPAIRS OF EVERY DESCRIPTION
PROMPT RELIABLE MODERATE

73. Another trade found in Ashford at the beginning of this century was the manufacture of bicycles. Allen is thought not to have manufactured them, but only to have assembled parts made elsewhere.

74.   The premises next to Allen Bros. served as a draper's shop for most of the 18th century. During the Napoleonic Wars more than 2,000 troops were stationed in Ashford and the building became a mess for army officers until 1819, when it became a baker's shop. This photograph shows the shop towards the end of the 19th century, when it was occupied by an ironmonger.

C. HAYWARD,
MANUFACTURER of the "ONWARD" CYCLE,
32, NEW STREET,
ASHFORD, KENT.

Cycles of every Description
Made to Order.
PLATING AND ENAMELLING DONE ON
THE PREMISES.
Fittings and Sundries of all kinds
kept in Stock.
REPAIRS IN ALL ITS BRANCHES
PROMPTLY EXECUTED.

75. Charles Hayward started his business in Castle Street, but moved to larger premises in New Street in 1895. From cycles he, his sons and grandsons progressed to motor cars, and the business (transferred to Caffyns Ltd. in 1967) has recently moved from New Street.

76. Two new trades of the 19th century were photography and local journalism. In Ashford early photography was developed by three brothers, sons of James Barns, a cabinetmaker who lived at 8 Middle Row. Around 1858 the youngest son, John, only 16 years old, started a business and was joined a few years later by his brother Samuel. By 1870 John had moved to Tenterden, where he continued as a photographer until his death in 1886. Samuel kept the Ashford business at 100 High Street until he died in 1889. The business was continued for a few years by his widow Mary, but when she remarried it passed to Hugh Penfold, who remained active until after the last war.

The eldest Barns brother Thomas (left), went into his father's trade, moving to 39 High Street c.1858. Later he moved to Faversham, where he was a photographer until the beginning of this century.

Henry Igglesden, born in Dover, came to Ashford in 1847 as a bookseller and printer. In 1855, following the repeal of the newspaper tax, he started the first Ashford newspaper, the first penny paper in Kent. At first titled *Ashford and Alfred News*, it became the *Kentish Express* in 1858. Henry Igglesden married the eldest sister of the Barns brothers.

77. After the First World War another cycle firm was established in the town by two brothers, Charles and Fred Norman. The firm was at first entitled the 'Kent Plating and Enamelling Company', with premises in Castle Street. In the early 1930s they had larger premises in Victoria Road and then, just before the war, a large new factory in Beaver Road, seen in this photograph.

78. By 1946 the factory was producing not only pedal cycles but motor cycles. These included the lightweight 'Norman Nippy' and more powerful machines. The advertisement shows the image the firm wished to present in 1961, by which time the original owners had sold the business to Tube Investments Ltd. The works were closed a few years later.

GIVE ME NORMAN

says Derek Minter—"I RIDE THEM—I KNOW"

Minter, first man to lap the famous Isle of Man T.T. circuit at over 100 m.p.h. on a British machine, knows what's required of a real motor cycle. Everything about it must be right; brakes, engine, looks, *feel.* The one he chooses for *himself* is—Norman!

It looks right, it feels right, it is right! The new B4 250 c.c. Sports Twin features high compression cylinder heads, sports handlebars and screen, new, exciting Italian red tank.

£192.0.0 INC. P.T.

New for 1961 is the range of B4 models, in roadster, sports and competitions trim. A redesigned cantilever frame gives hairline handling. Bend-swinging on a summer's day, or path-picking in winter wet, you're always in command — with *balanced* power — at the twist of a wrist from the 250 c.c. Villiers twin engine, individually tuned.

The B4 250 c.c. twin roadster has the same new frame as the Sports Twin but with easy-to-clean rear enclosure in the modern manner.
£192.0.0 INC. P.T.

'Leaders in the Lightweight class'

NORMAN

A COMPANY OF THE CYCLE DIVISION
NORMAN CYCLES LTD., ASHFORD, KENT

79. Another important local trade was tanning. A tannery is known to have existed at the 'Whist' since the early 16th century, and by the end of the next century the Greenhill family had acquired the business and premises. They continued for nearly 200 years, and were replaced by Dorman. The trade continued until the 1950s. This winter scene shows Whist House, in Tannery Lane, originally built in the 16th century, but with a new façade dated 1707.

80. Middle Row, *c.*1910, showing some of the trades being practised in Ashford at that time.

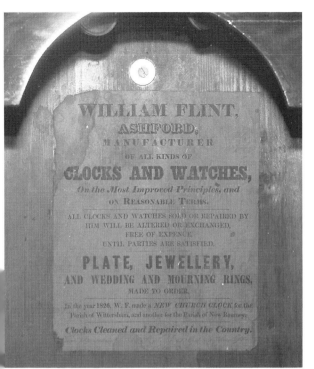

81-83. Clocksmiths settled in Ashford from an early date. They included Thomas Deale in the 17th century, and John Wimble in the next. Above left is one of Wimble's clocks, dating from *c.*1730. In 1790 William Flint came to Ashford from Charing to open a watch and clockmaker's shop at 60 High Street. He died in 1813, but the business was continued by his son William. An advertisement can be seen above right, with an example of his work (left). Although he described himself as a manufacturer he, like nearly all his provincial fellow tradesmen, bought the movements from a large-scale maker, assembling and casing them himself. He retired *c.*1858.

84. A view of Middle Row, with Rabson's at 53-55 High Street. They had shops in the town from about 1743 until recently, selling a variety of goods.

85. Another view of Rabson's in Middle Row taken early this century.

86. Greengrocery at 13 Middle Row, *c*.1903.

87.   Lower High Street, *c.*1910.

88.   Harper's furniture shop, 8-10 Castle Street, in the late 19th century.

89. Knott's general store , 39 Queen Street. This shop was owned by John Knott, and then by his widow, from the beginning of this century until about 1925.

90. This shop is probably 39 High Street, photographed *c*.1880.

91. These two old buildings, 77-79 High Street, were replaced in the last century. No. 77, on the left of the photograph, had to be rebuilt in 1884 after a fire.

92. This photograph, *c.*1870, shows John Howland's grocery at 12 Bank Street. He later expanded his premises to include nos. 14 and 16 too.

INNS AND INNKEEPERS

93.   The *George*, just seen on the right of this photograph taken at the beginning of the century, is the only ancient Ashford inn still trading in the original buildings, used about 500 years earlier. In his will of 1533 John Burwashe left the tenement called the *George* with three acres of land to his wife Idev. This land, behind the shops in the upper High Street, belonged to the *George* until the last century.

94.   The *Saracen's Head* stands on land which was owned by the lord of the manor until *c*.1800, and is probably the site of the original manor house. It is said that inns with this name originally had an actual head of a Saracen as the inn sign; the lord of the manor in the late 13th century did die fighting in the Crusades, and his followers could conceivably have brought such a trophy back to Ashford. The building shown in this photograph was erected in 1861, and was larger than its predecessor, which did not extend as far as the junction with North Street. This building was demolished in 1967.

95. This picture of the upper High Street must date from before 1873, because by then the *Fountain* Inn had been demolished. The inn was only known as the *Fountain* between 1840 and 1873; from at least the end of the 17th century it was called the *White Hart*.

96 & 97. These two photographs show a very old inn in North Street, called the *Red Lion* until the beginning of this century (left), and then the *Lord Roberts* (below), after the British general of the Boer War. It has now been demolished to make way for the new road.

98 & 99.   Bowketts was the *King's Head* Inn during the 18th century and was used for a time as the post office. That the two houses adjoining, now 69-71 High Street, were originally one is obvious from the rear, but the front of no. 71 has been rebuilt. These premises were also an inn during the 18th century, called the *Bull* (not to be confused with the *Pied Bull*, which was at 75 High Street) and previously the *Naked Boy* and the *Star*. In the mid-18th century the landlord was John Taylor, and he advertised in the *Kentish Post* that cockfights would be held at the *Bull*.

100. This photograph shows 31 High Street, occupied by George Edbrooke, a tailor, from *c*.1890. Earlier it had been the home of two generations of the Dorman family, tanners of the Whist, but during the 17th century it was yet another inn – the *Ounce's Head*. The unusual name is derived from the ounce or snow leopard, part of the armorial device of the Lords Strangford, lords of the manor of Ashford from 1558.

101. There is no evidence that Ashford ever had a castle, but the *Castle* Inn, at the corner of the High Street and New Rents, taken early this century, goes back to at least the 17th century, although for a number of years it was known as the *King's Head*.

102. The *New Inn*, opened about 1820, was one of five trading in New Street in the last century. Its appearance was later substantially altered by the addition of a mock timber-framed frontage.

103.   Another view of the *New Inn* which shows the area after bombing during the last war. The inn was subsequently demolished.

104. The *British Volunteer*, 56-58 New Street, was given that name in about 1865. The smaller *Bricklayers' Arms* occupied only no. 56 before that date. This photograph must have been taken in 1870, since John Moore, whose name can be seen on the sign, was landlord there for only a few years.

105. In the middle of the last century and only eight doors away was the *Rose and Crown* at 74 New Street. After about fifteen years it was renamed the *Greyhound*.

106. There were several inns on the outskirts of town such as the *Star*, on East Hill, with its unusual inn sign.

107. The *Old Prince of Wales* was a public house only from the middle of the last century, although about a hundred years earlier there had been a cider works on the site. The tank seen in this picture was presented to the town in 1919. For many years it housed an electricity sub-station.

108. Another picture of the tank, taken *c*.1972 before the protective covering was erected in 1987.

109. The *Queens Head* Inn at East Mill, about 1952.

PUBLIC SERVICES

110. During the 17th and 18th centuries most of the Ashford postmasters were innkeepers, since they were able to provide the necessary horses and stabling. In 1818 John Tunbridge was appointed postmaster, and continued as such until 1861. He was a furniture and general dealer, and had premises at 41 High Street (now part of Midland Bank). He was followed by John Edward Munns, whose premises were at 47-49 High Street, seen on the right, at the end of the century and occupied by Stevenson.

111 & 112. In 1870 Munns built a new house in Bank Street and moved there with the post office. The building was used until 1921, when the first purpose-built post office in Tufton Street (still in use) was opened. The photographs above show the post office in Bank Street, and (left) the same building used as a bank; today it is the National Westminster Bank.

113. This view of the bank after it had moved across the road to 81 High Street dates from *c*.1875.

114. The Bank Street frontage some years later.

115.   This building in the High Street was the Ashford Bank from the end of the 18th century until *c*.1845. The site, as far as 87 High Street, and the land fronting to Bank Street where the post office was built, was given for the upkeep of the church by Sir John Fogge in 1490. The photograph shows the premises at the beginning of this century, occupied by Walter Geering, printer, stationer and bookseller. Ashford Bank later moved to the building on the site now occupied by Lloyds Bank, who took over the Ashford Bank in 1902.

116. Complete rebuilding was carried out in 1925-6, resulting in the premises seen here *c*.1960.

117. The last member of the Jemmett family to manage the private bank was William Francis Bond Jemmett. He became the first manager of the branch of Lloyds Bank, when it took over in 1902.

118 & 119.   In 1836 the Kent, Surrey and Sussex Bank was formed and in 1840, now called the London and County Banking Company, they opened a branch in Ashford. Within a few years they moved to 20 High Street, and their successors, National Westminster Bank, have a branch there today. The photographs show (left) the building in the 19th century, and (below) c.1930.

120. The Ashford Trustee Savings Bank was started in this building, 25 High Street – with the Kent 'Invicta' badge. It was managed by Thomas Thurston, better known as a surveyor, but was badly affected by the opening of the Post Office Savings Bank in 1859, and closed in 1891. The minimum deposit in the Trustee Bank was 1 shilling, but this was too high for many working people. To meet the need a Penny Bank (accepting deposits of this amount) was started in 1859, run by the same managers, and closing at the same time.

121. Sir John Furley, born in Ashford, was responsible for promoting the establishment of first aid and ambulance services throughout the country and abroad. It is not surprising, therefore, that Ashford had one of the first St John's Ambulance detachments. This photograph shows one of their first motor ambulances, c.1920.

122. Ashford had one of the earliest organised volunteer fire brigades. This photograph was taken early in the 20th century.

123. This photograph was taken in 1925 and shows the Ashford Fire Brigade, under the leadership of their chief officer Captain G. E. Hart with their newly delivered Leyland engine.

124.   Late 19th-century fire fighting equipment and team.

125.   There was a town pump in the High Street for many years, and in 1864 this was supplemented by the drinking fountain seen in this photograph, presented to the town by Robert Furley, solicitor and historian.

126. Part of the sewage disposal works built in 1888. The name of the maker, Frederick Clark of Ashford, can be clearly seen.

127. Clark's works were near the market entrance, later demolished to make way for the ring road.

ELWICK IRON WORKS, ASHFORD.

FREDERICK CLARK,

Engineer, Millwright, Boiler Maker,

IRON AND BRASS FOUNDER,

Manufacturer of and Agent for Agricultural Implements,

STEAM PLOUGHING & THRASHING MACHINERY.

Agricultural Implements supplied at the several Makers' Prices.

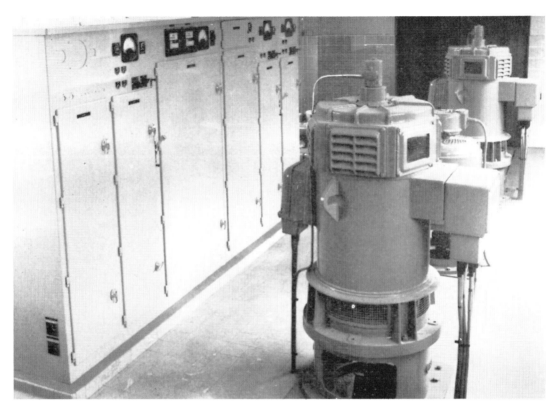

128 & 129.   The main sewage works remained in use for many years, although extensions were made to cope with the increased demand. By 1958 there were regular complaints from the residents about the smell coming from the works. With the possibility of substantial population expansion as a result of an agreement with the London County Council, new works were again urgently required. After public enquiries, the construction of new works was started on the same site. These photographs, dating from 1962, show the new pumping station, with much more modern machinery, and this time not manufactured in the town.

TRANSPORT

130. A horse bus in the upper High Street at the beginning of the present century.

131. Another horse-drawn vehicle in the lower High Street early this century.

132. Later motor vehicles in the lower High Street, in the 1920s.

The Fountain, High Street, Ashford.

133 & 134.   In 1836 the South Eastern Railway Company was formed to build a line from London to the south coast. When the necessary Act was debated in Parliament, there was opposition to the construction of another route in the capital and the new company was forced to make arrangements with the London and Brighton Company to use their tracks from Redhill to London. The Ashford station was opened on 1 December 1842. With the completion of the line to the coast, and branches to Canterbury, Thanet and Hastings, Ashford became an important junction. The above picture shows the station at the beginning of the century, and the other was taken c.1950. Very little has changed except for the locomotive hauling the boat express.

135. In 1846 the company decided to make Ashford the centre for their main construction works. They bought 185 acres of land from James Wall for £21,000, and the first superintendent, James L'Anson Cudworth, was appointed. He resigned in 1876, after a disagreement with the board of directors.

136. This photograph shows the entrance to the works in 1972. The next seven photographs show various operations at the works early this century. The large scale of the work, building locomotives, carriages and wagons, can be seen.

137. The Saw Mill.

138. The Drilling and Bolt Shop.

139. The Wheel Shop.

140. The Erecting Shop.

141.   Locomotive No. 31407.

142.   Building locomotives at the railway works.

143. Coach Shop.

144. This photograph of the Duke and Duchess of York (later King George VI and Queen Elizabeth) was taken during an official visit to Ashford in 1926. On the same day the new hospital in King's Avenue was opened.

145. The large numbers of people with special skills that had to be recruited for the works meant a great influx from other parts of the country – the census of 1851 showed that only a third of the inhabitants had been born in Ashford, and over 20 per cent came from outside Kent. The railway company built 72 cottages in 1847, the beginning of the estate called by them 'Alfred', but soon known as 'Newtown'. Additional houses were built, as well as a shop, public baths, a public house and other amenities.

146. The post office at Newtown. Note the sign reading 'Alfred Supply Stores'.

147. Newtown water tower and the *Alfred Arms*, 1972.

148. In 1852 this school, with places for 550 pupils, was provided by the company, *c.*1910.

149.   Development at Newtown continued throughout the last century, with additional houses being provided. Two of these were for the top management of the works, 'Belmont' and 'Alfred'. This photograph, taken c.1950, shows Belmont, erected c.1890 and occupied firstly by James Stirling, chief engineer from 1880 until 1899. It was then occupied by John Masterton, who was chief clerk. Alfred was the home of William Wainwright, superintendent of the carriage works and then by Harry Smith Wainwright who succeeded Stirling as chief engineer. Both houses were later converted into flats, and demolished c.1960.

CHURCHES AND CHAPELS

150. Ashford had a church before the Norman Conquest, but there was substantial reconstruction, including the building of the tower, towards the end of the 15th century. Internal changes made during the Commonwealth were not reversed until the very end of the 17th century, and additional seating was provided in the 18th century.

151. St Mary's church, pre 1830.

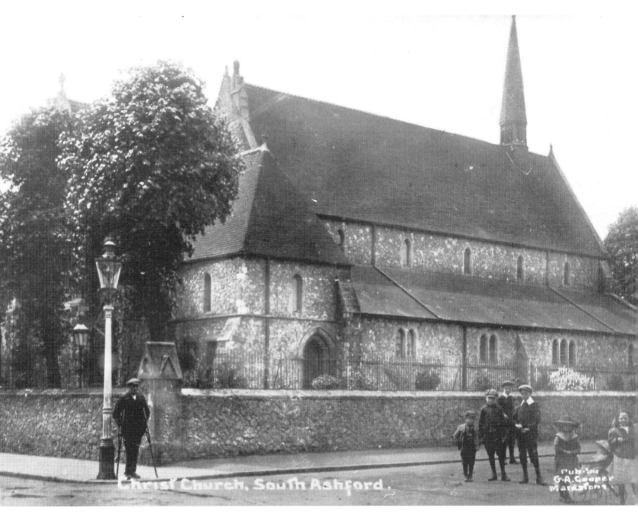

Christ Church, South Ashford.

Pub. by
G.A. Cooper
Maidstone

152.   The railway company appointed a chaplain in the early years, but he appears to have had too forceful a character to please the directors, and he was relieved of his position in 1855. The company contributed to the subscriptions totalling £4,500 that were raised to meet the cost of Christ Church in Beaver Road. It was opened on 1 May 1867 but not formally consecrated until 8 July 1889.

153. Alterations made to the church around 1475 were at the expense of Sir John Fogge, whose tomb is seen here.

154. Lords of the manor from 1558 to 1765 were members of the Smythe family. This shows one of several family tombs.

155. A view of the church from the south, showing the old sundial.

156. A college of priests was also founded by Sir John Fogge, but was dissolved during the Reformation. Despite this the house of the vicar, seen here in 1972, is still known as the College. The northern wing was demolished in the mid-18th century.

157 & 158.   Ashford was strongly nonconformist during the 17th century, when there were congregations of Independents and Baptists. From early in the 18th century the Independents (later the Congregationalists) had a meeting place in St John's Lane, at the rear of 19 High Street. The actual building survived until it was destroyed by bombing during the last war, but had been used for other purposes since 1784 when it was sold. Two cottages at the north-east corner of the churchyard were then used as a meeting house for nearly 40 years. A new meeting house was built in Tufton Street in 1822, but this was replaced by another on the same site in 1866. It was demolished c.1973, the magistrates' court being built on the site. These photographs show the church at the beginning of the century. The sheep are on part of the vicarage glebe, which originally extended to Station Road, including the site of the car park and the old burial ground.

159 & 160. The Baptist church was in St John's Lane; the church may account for the name of the road. In 1881 the first small building was replaced by a new one fronting Station Road, partly on land that had been used by the church as a burial ground, together with the adjoining site that had for centuries been used by the parish firstly as a bridewell or prison, and then as a home for poor persons. The photograph above shows the original building; the other shows the church as it is today.

161. The church in Bank Street, taken at the end of the last century, was erected by the Methodists to replace the one in Hempstead Street.

162. With Ashford's nonconformist tradition it is not surprising that the Catholic Church had little support in the town. Only with the arrival of many workers after the building of the railway works was such a church needed. At first services were conducted by the priest of the Darell family at Calehill, near Little Chart. These were held in the house, now 111 New Street, which had been used as a school but is now a public house called *The Prince of Orange*. In 1859 the Church purchased land in Canterbury Road (on the corner with Hardinge Road) for the erection of a church and school. This was apparently thought too small and was sold, a new site at Barrow Hill being acquired. This photograph shows the church erected there and opened in 1865. The church was later extended, and other accommodation added. It has recently been demolished and a new church built.

163.   The Wesleyan Methodists had a following in Ashford from the late 18th century, and in 1810 they bought a building
in Hempstead Street, adapting it as a chapel (foreground). In 1843 Elizabeth, the wife of William Betts, one of the major
contractors for the building of the railway, persuaded her husband to build a new chapel. Unfortunately she died before
it was completed, but it was used by the Methodists until 1875, when the move to Bank Street was made. This building
was then used by the Unitarian Church until about 1893. In 1898 the chapel was bought by the Society of Friends as their
meeting house. The Friends remained there until 1957. After that it became a furniture store, and it was finally demolished
in the 1970s to make way for the Tufton Centre.

SCHOOLS AND CHARITIES

164. Ashford Grammar School was endowed by Sir Norton Knatchbull in 1635, and a school house (now the Ashford Museum) erected. This is shown here, and was used until 1870. A large house to the north of the school, fronting the High Street, was used to accommodate the headmaster and the boarders. The school was closed for a few years until 1877, when a new scheme was approved by the Charity Commissioners, and a school erected in Hythe Road. This was used until 1958 when new buildings adjoining it were built. The old school is now part of the North School.

165. On 2 May 1816 a meeting was held in the *Saracen's Head* of 'friends of the proposed Institution for the education of the poor children of the Parish of Ashford'. This school was to be run as a National Society, and it was resolved 'that the attendance of the children at the Parish Church was a point of indispensable necessity'. The first school was in Gravel Walk, on land owned by the parish and used partly as the workhouse. In 1841 land at Barrow Hill, owned by the parish church, was acquired for a new school, holding 440 pupils. This is the school seen in the photograph at the end of the last century.

166. Street parades have always been popular. This picture shows the British School well represented. The occasion could be the coronation of 1911.

167. In view of the nonconformist views of many of the townspeople, it is surprising that a school for their children was not provided earlier. Not until 1840 was a British School opened, the original building being in Forge Lane. In 1862 it was succeeded by buildings in West Street, which are shown here. The school closed *c*.1930, and the premises were then used by the Salvation Army.

168. The growing population of the late Victorian period led to demands for more leisure facilities. A proposal to purchase land was first made in 1882, but deferred on several occasions. Not until 1898 was the land for Victoria Park bought from Jemmett for £2,780. This photograph dates from *c*.1902.

169. Ashford Grammar School, first founded by Sir Norton Knatchbull in 1636, went into a decline and finally closed in 1880. After a few years new trustees were appointed, and funds raised for the erection of this new school in Hythe Road, photographed at the end of the last century. The premises are now part of the North School for Boys.

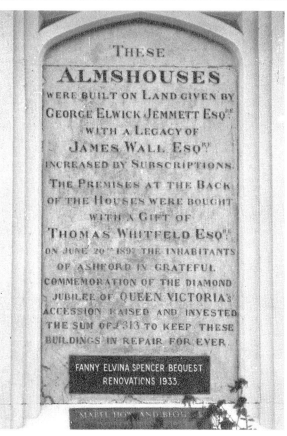

THESE
ALMSHOUSES
WERE BUILT ON LAND GIVEN BY
GEORGE ELWICK JEMMETT ESQ.
WITH A LEGACY OF
JAMES WALL ESQ.
INCREASED BY SUBSCRIPTIONS.
THE PREMISES AT THE BACK
OF THE HOUSES WERE BOUGHT
WITH A GIFT OF
THOMAS WHITFELD ESQ.
ON JUNE 20TH 1897 THE INHABITANTS
OF ASHFORD IN GRATEFUL
COMMEMORATION OF THE DIAMOND
JUBILEE OF QUEEN VICTORIA'S
ACCESSION RAISED AND INVESTED
THE SUM OF £313 TO KEEP THESE
BUILDINGS IN REPAIR FOR EVER.

FANNY ELVINA SPENCER BEQUEST
RENOVATIONS 1933.

170 & 171. Unlike many old towns, Ashford had no ancient foundation of almshouses for the poor. Four cottages were provided in 1855 in Tufton Street (opposite the Post Office) by public gifts and subscriptions. They were demolished to make way for the Tufton Centre, and were photographed in 1972.

172.   The Royal Cinema de Luxe was opened on 24 July 1912, and claimed to be the most luxurious in the district, and was built by Mr. E. J. Taylor, BA (Oxon) – a qualification which he was anxious to have acknowledged on every possible occasion – to compete with the Palace. He wanted to use the building on Sundays for concerts 'in keeping with the Sabbath', but the necessary licence was refused by the magistrates. The photograph shows the building about 1920, clearly decorated for some special occasion.

173.   The first cinema in Ashford was the Picture Palace in Tufton Street (on the site now occupied by a furniture store) which had opened on 18 December 1911. The first known purpose-built cinema had been opened in Lancashire in 1908, so Ashford was amongst the earliest. This view dates from the 1920s.

174.   The Drill Hall in Norwood Street – now replaced by the new police station. This photograph was probably taken at the beginning of the First World War.

172. The Royal Cinema de Luxe was opened on 24 July 1912, and claimed to be the most luxurious in the district, and was built by Mr. E. J. Taylor, BA (Oxon) – a qualification which he was anxious to have acknowledged on every possible occasion – to compete with the Palace. He wanted to use the building on Sundays for concerts 'in keeping with the Sabbath', but the necessary licence was refused by the magistrates. The photograph shows the building about 1920, clearly decorated for some special occasion.

173. The first cinema in Ashford was the Picture Palace in Tufton Street (on the site now occupied by a furniture store) which had opened on 18 December 1911. The first known purpose-built cinema had been opened in Lancashire in 1908, so Ashford was amongst the earliest. This view dates from the 1920s.

174. The Drill Hall in Norwood Street – now replaced by the new police station. This photograph was probably taken at the beginning of the First World War.

175.   The occasion of this photograph is unknown, but is a reminder of times when life was more leisurely than today.

The Learning Centre
K College
Jemmett Road
Ashford, Kent TN23 2RJ
Tel: 01233 655573
Email: **ashfordlrc@kcollege.ac.uk**